ISBN 978-0-365-16211-7
PIBN 11266521

For support please visit www.forgottenbooks.com

1 MONTH OF
FREE
READING

at

www.ForgottenBooks.com

By purchasing this book you are eligible for one month membership to ForgottenBooks.com, giving you unlimited access to our entire collection of over 1,000,000 titles via our web site and mobile apps.

To claim your free month visit:

www.forgottenbooks.com/free1266521

English
Français
Deutsche
Italiano
Español
Português

www.forgottenbooks.com

Mythology Photography **Fiction**
Fishing Christianity **Art** Cooking
Essays Buddhism Freemasonry
Medicine **Biology** Music **Ancient
Egypt** Evolution Carpentry Physics
Dance Geology **Mathematics** Fitness
Shakespeare **Folklore** Yoga Marketing
Confidence Immortality Biographies
Poetry **Psychology** Witchcraft
Electronics Chemistry History **Law**
Accounting **Philosophy** Anthropology
Alchemy Drama Quantum Mechanics
Atheism Sexual Health **Ancient History**
Entrepreneurship Languages Sport
Paleontology Needlework Islam
Metaphysics Investment Archaeology
Parenting Statistics Criminology
Motivational

Historic, archived document

Do not assume content reflects current
scientific knowledge, policies, or practices.

perative

NOMIC INSECT

ORT

by

'EST CONTROL DIVISION

TURAL RESEARCH SERVICE

STATES DEPARTMENT OF AGRICULTURE

AGRICULTURAL RESEARCH SERVICE

PLANT PEST CONTROL DIVISION

SURVEY AND DETECTION OPERATIONS

The Cooperative Economic Insect Report is issued weekly as a service to American Agriculture. Its contents are compiled from information supplied by cooperating State, Federal, and industrial entomologists and other agricultural workers. In releasing this material the Division serves as a clearing house and does not assume responsibility for accuracy of the material.

All reports and inquiries pertaining to this release, including the mailing list, should be sent to:

Survey and Detection Operations
Plant Pest Control Division
Agricultural Research Service
United States Department of Agriculture
Federal Center Building
Hyattsville, Maryland 20782

Volume 19   August 15, 1969   Number 33

COOPERATIVE ECONOMIC INSECT REPORT

HIGHLIGHTS

Current Condtions

ARMYWORM damage continues in South Dakota, Iowa, Minnesota, Wisconsin, and some areas of Nebraska. CORN EARWORM adult emergence increasing, could indicate pending outbreak in Virginia; adults increasing in blacklight traps in Maryland; abundant in Delaware. (pp. 637-638).

GREENBUG near economic levels on sorghum in some areas of Nebraska; increasing slowly in untreated sorghum in Oklahoma. (pp. 638-639).

MEXICAN BEAN BEETLE damaged beans in north-central Colorado and some controls applied in southeastern Wyoming. (p. 644).

MOSQUITOES expected to increase in Maryland; declined in Wisconsin and Minnesota. (p. 649).

GRASSHOPPERS defoliated white oak, hickory, and dogwood in Missouri; heavy on pines in California; heavy in some crop areas of Nebraska. (p. 650).

Detection

New State records include a WEEVIL in Arizona (p. 651) and a DERMESTID BEETLE in New Mexico (p. 649).

For new county records see page 651.

Special Reports

Distribution of Brown Recluse Spider (map). (p. 654).

CONTENTS

WEATHER OF THE WEEK ENDING AUGUST 11

HIGHLIGHTS: Summer heat continued in the West while more comfortable temperatures prevailed in the East. Isolated light showers fell in parts of the West. In the East, scattered thundershowers occurred early in week with heavier, more general rains over the weekend. Killer tornadoes struck Minnesota and Ohio.

PRECIPITATION: A slow-moving cold front, which moved from the Appalachian ridge to the Atlantic coast, produced some generous showers and thunderstorms along the Atlantic seaboard early in the week. About 3 inches of rain fell at Chattanooga, Tennessee, in 1 hour Tuesday evening. At midweek, a cold front edged into the northern Great Plains. Some killer tornadoes occurred in Minnesota Wednesday afternoon. The tornadoes killed 15 persons, injured many, and caused property damage estimated at $5 million. Up to 5 inches of rain fell 6 miles south of Crookston, Minnesota, and hail 1 inch in diameter caused total damage to crops 10 miles northeast of Hillsboro, North Dakota. A band of showers with a mixture of turbulent weather occurred from Michigan to Kansas. The weekend brought more violent weather to parts of mid-America. Severe thunderstorms, some with hail or heavy showers, and a few tornadoes occurred across Indiana and Ohio Saturday night. One of the worst left a path of destruction 0.25 mile wide and 7 miles long in the Cincinnati area on Saturday. It killed 4 persons, injured 235, and caused property damage estimated at $7 million.

TEMPERATURES: The warming trend in the Far Northwest continued after a brief interruption early in the week. Afternoon temperatures in Montana, in the 90's on Monday, dropped to the 70's and 80's on Tuesday, but climbed to the upper 90's by Sunday reaching 99° at Havre. Sweltering heat continued in the desert Southwest. On Monday afternoon, Palm Springs, California, registered 121°, the hottest temperature in the Nation so far in 1969. Maximums in parts of the desert averaged above 110°. Much of the area from southern California to the central and southern Rocky Mountains averaged several degrees above normal. Southerly winds warmed mid-America early and late in the week with maximums in the 90's from the Dakotas to Oklahoma and above 100° over most of Texas by Sunday when Waco registered 109°. Near seasonal temperatures prevailed over most of the East. Temperatures were especially pleasant over the Northeast where some warmup occurred at midweek followed by a cool comfortable weekend. Temperatures from Alabama to South Carolina averaged a few degrees cooler than normal. (Summary supplied by Enviromental Data Service, ESSA.)

SPECIAL INSECTS OF REGIONAL SIGNIFICANCE

ARMYWORM (Pseudaletia unipuncta) - WYOMING - About 70 acres of oats and alfalfa treated in Goshen County. (Skelton). Moving into homes at Torrington, Goshen County. (Parshall). NEBRASKA - Economic in Keith County, some control activity. (Raun). Six per square foot in corn rows, some injury to lower corn leaves in one field in Merrick County. (Roselle). SOUTH DAKOTA - Continues to damage crops and gardens in State. Some degree of infestation in all counties east of Missouri River. Damaged crops now include flax. New areas west of Missouri River reported near Hot Springs, Fall River County, and at Sturgis, Meade County. Southeastern areas, in southern Lincoln County, observed feeding on silks of corn; no estimate of damage made, although 20 percent of ears with silks contained larvae, and ranged second to fifth instar. (Jones, Kantack). NORTH DAKOTA - Scattered in west-central and southwest counties. Infestations in hail-damaged areas; numbers highest where hail damage most severe. On 1,280-1,920 acre area near Killdeer, ranged 3 per square foot in wheat to 30 per square foot in oats. Larvae 60 per square foot in margins of some adjacent corn and oatfields. Severest damage occurred to oats where 100 percent of leaves stripped in parts of some fields. Corn also damaged, 20 rows from edge in Dunn County. Larvae ranged 2-30 per square foot in 3-4 township areas near Lefor; oats, barley, wheat, and millet main crops damaged. Larvae feeding on heads after stripping leaves in some oat and wheatfields. Also, swathed oats, cut for hay, had up to 80 larvae per square foot under windrows. Up to 90 percent of oat kernels clipped in Stark and Hettinger Counties. Larvae ranged 3-30 per square foot in 6 township areas south of Beach in oat and wheatfields; 90 percent of plants defoliated in some fields in Golden Valley County. In all areas crops are regrowth from hail damage and in flower to milk stage of development. Larvae vary in size from less than half inch to 1.5 inch. Controls applied and effective. (Brandvik).

MINNESOTA - Armyworm remains major insect problem in State. Appearing farther north; spotty in Stearns, Meeker, Kandiyohi, Chippewa, and Swift Counties, highest in weedy oat and cornfields. Light and scattered, not economic, in Douglas, Grant, and Wilkin Counties. Heads clipped on swathed grain throughout southern area; spraying before combining required in some fields. Alfalfa and other legumes "seeded-down" with small grain damaged in some southwestern counties after grain harvest; some fields sprayed. Damaged mostly weedy corn in Rock, Pipestone, Nobles, and Wright Counties; damage severe in some fields. Oat losses in southwestern area ranged 10-60 percent. Heavy; damaged about 5,000 acres, with about 1,000 acres sprayed in Chippewa County. High numbers picked up in swath and plugging sieves in combines in southwest district. Some storage bins topped with crawling larvae. Problem not over; expected to become more evident in corn with larval growth and migration. Many full-grown larvae and pupae but all sizes present and feeding. (Minn. Pest Rpt.). IOWA - About 5 percent pupating July 30 in Lyon County; 30-50 percent smaller than 1 inch. In 1 square mile of corn, half of field damaged; only stalks and midribs remain in 100-150 acres. (Iowa. Ins. Inf.). ILLINOIS - Outbreak about over. (Sur. Bull). WISCONSIN - Controls applied in Walworth, Fond du Lac, and Lafayette Counties and to 1,000 acres of oats in Dodge County and about 1,300 acres in Grant County. Peas and sweet corn treated in Rock and Walworth Counties. Damage ranged from total loss of some grain fields in Dodge County to stripping of seedings in Grand and Lafayette Counties. Larvae ranged 40 per square foot and 45 per corn plant to less than 1 per 10 row foot. Infestations often spotty and dependent upon site at time of oviposition. Larvae ranged about one-half inch to pupae; most about half grown. Parasitism less than 3 percent in all areas. Parasitism by a tachina fly, Winthemia quadripustulata, most noticeable; few cocoon masses of Apanteles militaris in spots. Diseased larvae numerous in some fields but less than 10 percent in most. Pea harvest essentially over and where controls applied early enough results favorable. Corn seldom if ever damaged too severely. (Wis. Ins. Sur.). MICHIGAN - Reported feeding on field corn last period. Problem on field corn very mild, except for few fields. Bacterial disease beginning to take some of larger larvae. (Janes, Aug. 4). Recovered 210 moths in blacklight traps in Lenawee, Livingston, and Berrien Counties. (Newman, Aug. 4). INDIANA - Adult catches in blacklight traps low in all districts from July 28 to August 1:

Southwest district 100, south-central 54, east-central 80, central 74, northwest 81. (Huber). OHIO - Armyworm damage moderate to lawns at Bryan, Williams County. (Phillips, Jones).

ASTER LEAFHOPPER (Macrosteles fascifrons) - WISCONSIN - Appears static in northeastern area carrot plantings. Ranged about 3 per foot near margin to 1 per 10 feet farther into field. Aster yellows remains low. (Wis. Ins. Sur.).

CORN EARWORM (Heliothis zea) - NEW YORK - Moth catches at Poughkeepsie, Hudson Valley area approaching 1 per night in spite of rains. Most sweet corn silks treated. On untreated mid to late silk at Poughkeepsie, 100 tips yielded 8 larvae of first to third instar July 31. On August 3, infestation level of 12 percent with instars up to fourth. (N.Y. Wkly. Rpt., Aug. 4). DELAWARE - Adults very abundant in blacklight trap collections in Kent and Sussex Counties. (Burbutis, Kelsey). MARYLAND - Blacklight trap collections increasing on Eastern Shore. Damage to ears ranged 60-100 percent in all sections of Eastern Shore below Queen Annes County. (U. Md., Ent. Dept.). WEST VIRGINIA - Light damage to sweet corn in Lincoln County. Larvae 1 per ear on 10 ears. (Hacker). VIRGINIA - Moth emergence increasing and could indicate outbreak in near future. Expect increasing damage from mid-August to cool weather on Eastern Shore. (Hofmaster). GEORGIA - Moderate to heavy across peanut belt. (French, Hall, et al.). MISSOURI - Mostly second and third instars, light on sorghum in south-central area. Ranged 6-8 per 100 heads. (Hanning). NEW MEXICO - Damaged ears and light to severe in whorls of corn in southern counties. (N.M. Coop. Rpt.). ARIZONA - Larvae in corn and sorghum in Maricopa and Pinal Counties. Some fields treated. Heliothis zea 2-3 per ear of corn at Safford, Graham County. (Ariz. Coop. Sur.). WASHINGTON - Damage light to moderate in 1-acre tomato field at Pasco, Franklin County. (Hokanson).

CORN LEAF APHID (Rhopalosiphum maidis) - IDAHO - Large numbers in spring grain at Moore, Butte County, and in Pahsimeroi River Valley, Custer County. Lady beetle and syrphid larvae very numerous on August 3. (Portman). WYOMING - Averaged 24 percent of corn infested. Up to 2,000 per corn plant in Goshen, Laramie, Platte, and Converse Counties. Lady beetle adults and larvae numerous in most fields. (Parshall). COLORADO - Numerous in some cornfields in Weld, Boulder, Larimer, and Morgan Counties; tassels damaged. Noneconomic in fields checked. (Johnson). OKLAHOMA - Decreasing rapidly in Texas County. Ranged up to 400 per plant in occasional sorghum fields, most ranged 50-75 per plant. Ranged 50-200 per plant in Ellis County. (Okla. Coop. Sur.). ILLINOIS - Increasing on late whorl to early tassel corn in northern area; lightly infested average of 20 percent of plants. (Ill. Ins. Rpt.). WISCONSIN - Heavy in many cornfields in Waushara, Portage, Waupaca, and areas of sandy soils in northeast. (Wis. Ins. Sur.). MICHIGAN - Remains very low on corn fully tasseled. Occur on corn just coming into this condition, some show moderately sized colonies. Only on about 10 percent of plants. Possible increase on corn remaining to tassel. (Janes, Aug. 4). INDIANA - Colonies found in few fields which still had tassel in whorl stage corn in central districts. Less abundant this year than for at least 4 years. (Meyer). OHIO - Young colonies of 50-500 individuals per stalk appearing in northeastern area; most common on emerging tassels and between husks of ears. Winged adults few. Abundant parasites may provide satisfactory control. (Richter). MARYLAND - Negative on corn Statewide. (U. Md., Ent. Dept.).

GREENBUG (Schizaphis graminum) - SOUTH DAKOTA - On grain sorghum in western Bon Homme County, near Avon; and throughout Charles Mix County, from Wagner in south to north of Platte. On underside of lower leaves. Plants about 3.5 feet high. Averaged 100 per plant. Higher on individual plants where plants closer together. Predators, both Coccinellidae, late larvae and adults, and Neuroptera, present. Few winged greenbugs Present. Heaviest counts in field 3 miles west of Wagner. (Kvenberg). NEBRASKA - Variable, ranged 25 to 200 on each of lower 4 leaves of sorghum in Buffalo County, some colonies on stems; 50-600 per each of lower 5 leaves in Merrick County. Four fields in Lancaster County with only occasional colonies of 10-25 greenbugs on lower leaves. As many as 800 per leaf on few fields in Otoe County. (Roselle). Alate forms numerous in Hamilton County on

August 6. (Munson). Control activity in some locations. Damage and extent of
infestations less than at this time in 1968. Approaching economic numbers in
Keith County. (Raun). COLORADO - Greenbug light to moderate found on Western
Slope on sorghum. Controls may be necessary. (Fronk, Bulla). OKLAHOMA - Variable
in sorghum in Texas County. Some fields range 500-3,000 per plant, while others
range 0-200 per plant. Continues to increase slowly in untreated fields. (Okla.
Coop. Sur.). NEW MEXICO - Greenbug and Rhopalosiphum maidis (corn leaf aphid)
light to moderate in Union County sorghum. Greenbug light but present in almost
every field. (Zimmerman). Growers still treating grain sorghum in Luna and
Hidalgo Counties. (N.M. Coop. Rpt.).

POTATO LEAFHOPPER (Empoasca fabae) - MICHIGAN - Very low in central and southwest
areas. Highest counts 2 adults and 1 nymph per 100 sweeps of alfalfa. (Janes,
Aug. 4). OHIO - Adults barely economic, ranged 8-12 per sweep in northeastern
area alfalfa. Feeding damage light with few moderate and none severe. (Richter).
MARYLAND - None on alfalfa in Talbot, Dorchester, Wicomico, and Somerset Counties.
In western counties highest counts in 2-acre field, ranged 22-28 per sweep. Most
fields in central area negative. Appears below 1968 levels. (U. Md., Ent. Dept.).

POTATO PSYLLID (Paratrioza cockerelli) - WYOMING - Adults increasing in potato
fields of Goshen and Laramie Counties. Adults ranged 0-11 per 100 sweeps.
(Parshall).

SPOTTED ALFALFA APHID (Therioaphis maculata) - NEW MEXICO - Only minor in most
alfalfa. Apparent buildup with noticeable effects observed in one field near
Roswell, Chaves County. (Mathews).

TOBACCO HORNWORM (Manduca sexta) - WEST VIRGINIA - Light to moderate damage in
Lincoln and Mason Counties. Larvae 1-2 per plant on 10 plants. (Hacker).

CORN, SORGHUM, SUGARCANE

EUROPEAN CORN BORER (Ostrinia nubilalis) - NEW YORK - Moth catches at Hurley,
Hudson Valley area increased. Moths numerous in weedy field borders. One second
instar found in untreated silk tips on July 31. Erie County area hardest hit
than any of past 10 years. (N.Y. Wkly. Rpt., Aug. 4). NEW JERSEY - Second-
generation borers not expected to cause trouble in most cornfields in State.
(Ins.-Dis. Newsltr.). MARYLAND - Ranged 10-50 percent infested on sweet corn
ears in Dorchester, Wicomico,and Somerset Counties. Pupating on Eastern Shore;
adult emergence moderate in Talbot and Queen Annes County area (average 16 per
night). Second-generation larvae active in central counties. Infestations
expected to increase rapidly within next few weeks in all sections, with peak
first-generation moth flights coming. (U. Md., Ent. Dept.). VIRGINIA - Locally
severe on field of sudax in Albemarle County. Determined by J.O. Rowell,
(Lombard). Present in corn throughout State, generally noneconomic (Allen).
Third-brood moth emergence beginning and should peak around August 15. (Hofmaster).
OHIO - Generally below economic levels in northeastern area. Damaged nearly all
stalks in field in eastern Knox County; infested 30-50 percent of stalks in most
fields. (Richter). INDIANA - Second-generation adults taken in blacklight traps
during week July 28 to August 1: Southwest district 495, south-central 8, east-
central 21, central 19, northwest 32. (Huber). MICHIGAN - Present indications
that populations will be heavier than 1968. (Newman, Aug. 4). WISCONSIN - Heavy
in many areas with threat of even higher numbers upon emergence of first brood.
Flight of first-generation moths just starting in southern counties. Some first-
generation larvae beginning to enter ears in Outagamie County; very few in ear
tips in southern counties. Development at Hancock, Waushara County, 30 percent
fifth instar and 70 percent pupae; Janesville, Rock County, 15 percent third
instar, 42 percent fifth instar and 43 percent pupae; Hortonville, Outagamie
County, 60 percent third instars, 30 percent fourth instar, and 10 percent pupae;
Coleman, Marinette County, 50 percent second and third instars. Infested 80-100
percent of many fields even as far north as Oconto County. Third instars in 20
percent of sweet corn ears in field about 10 days from harvest. Control poorly
applied. (Wis. Ins. Sur.). ILLINOIS - First-generation pupation 20-40 percent in

northern area. Some egg masses. First generation completed. Larvae per 100 stalks
averaged 3.9 Statewide; by district: Northeast 11.2, west 6.7, northwest 4.7,
west-southwest 1.1, east 0.7, and west 0.5. Highest in Knox (11.2) and Ogle (8.4)
Counties. (Ill. Ins. Rpt.). Egg laying for second generation in southern area
nearly complete. Moth emergence near completion in central area. Egg laying should
peak in few weeks. Emergence in north area beginning. Egg masses few. First-
generation larvae pupating. (Sur. Bull.). MISSOURI - In north-central and northeast area 0-40 percent leaf feeding observed on 30-50 inch late-planted corn; egg
masses ranged 5-190 per 100 plants. Early planted corn 1-20 egg masses per 100
plants with 60-90 percent moth emergence. (Thomas). IOWA - Three random stops, 40
percent infested at Woodbury County (20 per 100 plants), 44 percent at Ida County
(110 borers per 100 plants), 40 percent infestation at Sac County (no borers,
pupae or larvae in 2 plots). (Iowa Ins. Inf.). MINNESOTA - Appear highest,
averaged 100 per 100 plants, in southwest district. Stalk breakage highest in
more advanced cornfields. Averaged 3 larvae per plant in some fields in Lac
qui Parle and Yellow Medicine Counties; development ranged second instar to pupae;
some emergence occurred. (Minn. Pest Rpt.).

FALL ARMYWORM (Spodoptera frugiperda) - ALABAMA - Larvae light to medium in sorghum-
sudan hybrids at Marion Junction in Dallas County. Older larvae pupated. (Smith).
VIRGINIA - Locally severe in one cornfield 90 percent affected in Sussex County.
Determined by J.O. Rowell. (Wright). MARYLAND - First instar larvae on 40 percent
of 10 acres of 8-inch high field corn near Motters, Frederick County. Averaged
20 percent on acre planting near Woodsboro. Statewide light and spotty. (U. Md.,
Ent. Dept.). WISCONSIN - Few nearly full-grown larvae feeding in whorls of field
corn in Rock County. (Wis. Ins. Sur.). MISSOURI - First to fourth instar larvae
ranged 1-17 per plant on 7-95 percent of corn 8-40 inches tall in north-central
area. (Hanning). OKLAHOMA - Moderate to heavy in corn and sorghum in northwest,
west-central, southwest, north-central, and central areas. Moderate to heavy in
broomcorn in Stephens County. (Okla. Coop. Sur.).

SOUTHWESTERN CORN BORER (Diatraea grandiosella) - MISSISSIPPI - Second-generation
emergence increasing in central areas, beginning in northern part of State. Populations high in Oktibbeha County. (Sartor). ARIZONA - Larvae in corn and sorghum in
Maricopa and Pinal Counties. Some fields treated. (Ariz. Coop. Sur.).

LESSER CORNSTALK BORER (Elasmopalpus lignosellus) - ARIZONA - Larvae in corn and
sorghum in Maricopa and Pinal Counties. Some fields treated. (Ariz. Coop. Sur.).

NORTHERN CORN ROOTWORM (Diabrotica longicornis) - WISCONSIN - Lodged some corn in
Pepin and Richland Counties; some light lodging in Rock County. Adults averaged 2
per silk on some Rock County corn with as high as 4 per silk. Estimated about half
emerged in Rock County August 1. Most adults still pale. (Wis. Ins. Sur.).
INDIANA - Adults ranged 0-50 per 10 silks in central districts; averaged 6 beetles
per 10 silks. Adults low this year, and silking well underway. (Meyer). MARYLAND -
First adults of season found feeding on corn silks near Emmitsburg, Frederick
County. Every ear infested in 12-acre stand. Adults also active in Carroll and
Howard Counties. Every ear infested in 15-acre field at Keymar, Carroll County.
(U. Md., Ent. Dept.).

WESTERN CORN ROOTWORM (Diabrotica virgifera) - IOWA - Adult counts 2, 0.5, and 1
per plant in Woodbury, Ida, and Sac Counties. (Iowa Ins. Inf.). WYOMING - Adults
0-16 per plant in southeastern area corn. Damaged silks in Goshen County field
where counts averaged 9 per plant. (Parshall).

CORN ROOTWORMS (Diabrotica spp.) - MINNESOTA - Adults more numerous; silk feeding
increasing but not serious. Peak emergence about 7 days away. Lodging spotty.
Highest in Wright County cornfield where 80 percent of plants lodged. Larvae in
soil but prepupae and pupae more common. (Minn. Pest Rpt.). ILLINOIS - D.
longicornis and D. virgifera adult emergence slow; 2-3 per plant common. (Ill.
Ins. Rpt.). OKLAHOMA - Adults emerging in heavy numbers in Texas County corn.
Most fields average 2-5 per plant. Averaged about 85 percent D. virgifera and
15 percent D. undecimpunctata howardi (southern corn rootworm). (Okla. Coop. Sur.).

CORN FLEA BEETLE (Chaetocnema pulicaria) - MARYLAND - Increasing on corn;
ranged 30-100 percent infested in Frederick County. (U. Md., Ent. Dept.).

GRASSHOPPERS (Melanoplus spp.) - MARYLAND - Ranged 10-70 percent defoliation of
border rows in corn in Frederick and Carroll Counties. (U. Md., Ent. Dept.).

BANKS GRASS MITE (Oligonychus pratensis) - NEBRASKA - Near economic numbers on
corn in panhandle counties. Some control in progress. (Hagen). WYOMING - Light
in all fields checked in southeastern area; only on bottom 1-2 leaves. (Parshall).

TWO-SPOTTED SPIDER MITE (Tetranychus urticae) - COLORADO - Increasing in northeastern areas. In some cornfields, fourth and fifth leaves infested. Controls
applied. (Johnson).

TURF, PASTURES, RANGELAND

GRASSHOPPERS - INDIANA - Populations in roadside grasses low through central
districts, ranged only occasionally to 5 per sweep. (Meyer). IOWA - Causing much
concern in southern third of State. (Iowa Ins. Inf.).

SOUTHERN CHINCH BUG (Blissus insularis) - ALABAMA - High numbers of all stages
damaging most St. Augustine grass lawns in Montgomery County. (McCabe et al.).

FORAGE LEGUMES

ARMYWORMS (Spodoptera spp.) - ARIZONA - S. exigua (beet armyworm) larvae 165 per
100 sweeps in alfalfa field at Yuma, Yuma County. (Ariz. Coop. Sur.). ARKANSAS -
S. frugiperda (fall armyworm) remains light to heavy in scattered areas. Economic
in one hayfield in Crawford County. Larvae ranged 300-400 in 100 sweeps in
alfalfa in north Logan County. (Boyer).

ALFALFA CATERPILLAR (Colias eurytheme) - WYOMING - Averaged 1 per 10 sweeps of
alfalfa in Niobrara, Laramie, and Converse Counties. (Parshall). NEW MEXICO -
Larvae averaged 15-40 per 25 sweeps in alfalfa checked in Roswell area, Chaves
County. (Mathews).

YELLOW-STRIPED ARMYWORM (Prodenia ornithogalli) - MISSOURI - Mixed larval
populations of this and Loxostege spp. (webworms) ranged from 15-40 per 10
sweeps on alfalfa in south-central area. (Hanning).

WEBWORMS (Loxostege spp.) - OKLAHOMA - Heavy in irrigated alfalfa in Grady County.
Averaged 2 per square foot in Kiowa County. Light in Ottawa County. (Okla. Coop.
Sur.).

ALFALFA WEEVIL (Hypera postica) - WISCONSIN - Infested estimated two-thirds of
alfalfa acreage in State. (Wis. Ins. Sur.).

ASIATIC OAK WEEVIL (Cyrtepistomus castaneus) - MISSOURI - One adult on partridge
peas in Howell County. Adults in Carter County alfalfa. These are new county
records. (Hanning).

CLOVER HEAD WEEVIL (Hypera meles) - MISSOURI - Adults on red clover and white
clover in Macon, Marion, and Ralls Counties. These are new county records.
(Hanning).

CLOVER SEED WEEVIL (Miccotrogus picirostris) - MISSOURI - Adults on white clover
and alsike clover in Lincoln, Pike, Macon, Marion, Howard, Chariton, and Monroe
Counties. These are new county records. (Hanning).

A JAPANESE WEEVIL (Calomycterus setarius) - MISSOURI - Collected for first time in Marion County on white clover. (Hanning).

A LEAF MINER FLY (Agromyza spiraeae) - MASSACHUSETTS - Moderate to heavy damage; averaged 1,297.8 per 100 sweeps in 4 alfalfa fields July 24 in Hamsphire County. (Miller).

GRASSHOPPERS - ILLINOIS - Abundant in many clover and alfalfa fields. (Sur. Bull.). MISSOURI - Ranged 0-53 per 10 sweeps on alfalfa in north-central area and ranged 10-60 per 10 sweeps in northeast area. (Thomas).

MEADOW SPITTLEBUG (Philaenus spumarius) - MISSOURI - Collected for first time in Chariton County. (Hanning).

LYGUS BUGS (Lygus spp.) - NEVADA - Varied 3-6 per sweep in Reese River, Lander County, alfalfa seed fields. Some stripping occurring. Ranged 1-3 per sweep with 8 per sweep in some alfalfa seed fields in Orovada, Humboldt County. (Hilbig, Aug. 1). ARIZONA - Average per 100 sweeps in alfalfa, 1 field each: lower Yuma County, 460; Casa Grande, Pinal County, 250; and Safford, Graham County, 79 adults and 59 nymphs. (Ariz. Coop. Sur.). WYOMING - Ranged 3-14 per 10 sweeps of southeastern area alfalfa. (Parshall). OHIO - L. lineolaris (tarnished plant bug) most common in northeastern area alfalfa, averaging 408 per 10 sweeps. (Richter).

PEA APHID (Acyrthosiphon pisum) - NEVADA - Very light in Reese River, Lander County, and Orovada, Humboldt County, alfalfa seed fields. (Hillbig, Aug. 1). WYOMING - Decreasing rapidly, 5-32 per 10 sweeps, on southeastern area alfalfa. (Parshall). MASSACHUSETTS - Averaged 1,179.5 per 100 sweeps in 4 alfalfa fields July 24 in Hampshire County. (Miller).

SOYBEANS

BEAN LEAF BEETLE (Cerotoma trifurcata) - ALABAMA - Heavy, high of 8 per row foot on soybeans in few fields in Dallas and Greene Counties. (Smith et al.).

STRIPED BLISTER BEETLE (Epicauta vittata) - MISSISSIPPI - Causing light damage to soybeans at State College, Oktibbeha County. (Sartor).

GREEN CLOVERWORM (Plathypena scabra) - ILLINOIS - Larvae common in many soybean fields but remain generally low, averaging 2 larvae per row foot. (Ill. Ins. Rpt.).

SPIDER MITES (Tetranychus spp.) - VIRGINIA - Severe on soybeans in several locations in Lancaster County. Determined by W.A. Allen. (McSwain).

PEANUTS

NOCTUID MOTHS - ALABAMA - Anticarsia gemmatalis (velvetbean caterpillar) first-generation larvae light in Covington County. (Pike). Feltia subterranea (granulate cutworm) larvae continue to damage peanuts in southeast area. (Estes et al.). Spodoptera exigua (beet armyworm) larvae very numerous in a 100+ acre peanut field in Barbour County. (Bond).

LESSER CORNSTALK BORER (Elasmopalpus lignosellus) - OKLAHOMA - Found in all dryland peanut fields checked in Garvin, Pontotoc, and Hughes Counties. Ranged less than 1-5 percent of plants damaged. (Okla. Coop. Sur.).

RED-NECKED PEANUTWORM (Stegasta bosqueella) - OKLAHOMA - Moderate in Bryan County peanuts. (Okla. Coop. Sur.).

COTTON

BOLL WEEVIL (Anthonomus grandis) - OKLAHOMA - Punctured square counts ranged up
to 80 percent in Kiowa County and up to 40 percent in Caddo County. Ranged 4-6
percent in Jackson, Marshall, and Bryan Counties. (Okla. Coop. Sur.). LOUISIANA -
Remains light in most Madison Parish fields. From 116 fields checked 113 infested,
averaged 3.5 (ranged 1-18) percent. Recovered 3 weevils from 10 wing traps
placed near hibernation sites. (Cleveland et al.). ARKANSAS - Out of 6,481 fields
checked, 4,384 or 68 percent infested; 1,459 or 22 percent above treatment level.
(Boyer, Barnes). TENNESSEE - Decreased as dry weather continues in western area.
Another "hatchout" expected in 7 days. Punctured squares 1-52 percent; some boll
injury in "cut out" fields. (Locke). MISSISSIPPI - Surveys in 11 western counties
indicate an increase over previous period. In 217 fields averaged 3-14 percent
infested. (Sartor). Punctured squares in 8 of 10 delta counties fields, averaged
3.6 (maximum 10) percent. In 28 sex lure traps collected 2; total to date 256.
(Pfrimmer et al.). ALABAMA - More widespread problem than previously existed in
northern areas. Controls not extensive. Overlapping generations with very high
numbers continue in south and central areas. Where controls regular and good, populations held to manageable numbers. Continues to puncture small bolls. (McQueen).
GEORGIA - Punctured squares ranged 1-16 (average 8.1) percent in 12 fields in
Randolph County, 7 percent in one field in Peach County, 12 percent in one field
in Worth County (Womack); 22-37 percent and increasing in Tift County (Canerday);
25 percent in Spalding County (Beckham). SOUTH CAROLINA - In Florence County
infestations increasing but below normal. (Taft et al.). For Boll Weevil in
High Plains see page 650.

BOLLWORMS (Heliothis spp.) - ARIZONA - H. zea damaged 50-60 squares and bolls
per 100 row feet at Safford, Graham County. Eggs and larvae averaged 0.226 per
100 terminals checked in 522 fields July 28 to August 2. Light at Casa Grande,
Pinal County, appearing in Maricopa County. (Ariz. Coop. Sur.). NEW MEXICO -
Mature larvae still found in bolls and squares in Luna, Dona Ana, Chaves, and
Eddy Counties. (N.M. Coop. Rpt.). TEXAS - Light in High Plains in Floyd, Howard,
Gaines, Lynn, Yoakum, Terry, and Scurry Counties. Light to medium in Dawson
County. (Almand, Clymer, Aug. 5). OKLAHOMA - Damaged square counts ranged up to
80 percent in Tillman County and up to 40 percent in Jackson County. Ranged
3-18 percent in Stephens, Marshall, and Kiowa Counties. Averaged 2 percent in
Grady County. (Okla. Coop. Sur.). MISSOURI - In 544 fields in southern areas
infested 169. (Jones). ARKANSAS - Of 6,481 fields, 515 had eggs only; 1,897 had
larvae only; and 1,825 had both eggs and larvae for total of 4,219 or 65 percent.
Square damage in 4,916 fields or 76 percent. Damaged squares ranged 5-8 percent
in 692 or 11 percent of fields; 488 or 7.5 percent with above 8 percent damaged
squares. Bollworms continue lower in northeast areas than in other areas. Small
larvae found on large bolls. (Boyer, Barnes). LOUISIANA - Damaged squares in 113
of 116 fields in Madison Parish; ranged 1-13 percent. In 84 of 95 fields
averaged 4 (ranged 1-11) percent damaged bolls. Larvae averaged 1.9 percent
in 19 fields. Collected 51 H. zea and 1 H. virescens moths from blacklight trap.
(Cleveland et al.). MISSISSIPPI - In delta counties injured squares in 10 of 10
fields; averaged 7.4 (maximum 21) percent. Eggs for next generation found; indicates overlapping of generations till frost. Large portion of larvae in field
H. virescens. In 95 sex lure traps collected 57 H. zea; total to date 2,853.
(Pfrimmer et al.). In 8 western counties increase indicated over last week. In
143 fields averaged 2-13.5 percent infested. (Sartor). TENNESSEE - Much damage
over western area; damage in all fields surveyed. All stages found. Egg laying
remains heavy on rank cotton. Eggs and larvae ranged 1-18 (averaged 3) per 100
terminals. (Locke). ALABAMA - General increase in moth flights with sharp rise in
larvae occurring in cotton throughout State. Ranged 15-30 larvae per 100 plants
where irregular or poor applications used for weevil control in past 15 days of
low larvae activity. (McQueen). GEORGIA - Eggs ranged 4-40 (average 13.7) and
larvae 4-32 (average 9.3) per 100 terminals in Randolph County (Womack); eggs
and larvae remain heavy in Tift County (Canerday); catches heavy in light traps
in Tift County (French). SOUTH CAROLINA - Infestations increasing in Florence
County and damaging unprotected fields. Collected in blacklight traps 1,461 H.
zea, total to date 2,543; and H. virescens 13, total to date 47. (Taft et al.).

CABBAGE LOOPER (Trichoplusia ni) - ARIZONA - Building up in some fields at Yuma, Yuma County; control difficult. Appearing in Pinal and Maricopa Counties. (Ariz. Coop. Sur.). OKLAHOMA - Damage moderate to cotton in Tipton area of Tillman County. (Okla. Coop. Sur.). TENNESSEE - Light in western area. (Locke). ALABAMA - Light in many cotton fields throughout State. Naturally developing virus disease occurring among larvae in several fields in central areas and may stop infestation. (McQueen).

BEET ARMYWORM (Spodoptera exigua) - GEORGIA - Light to moderate in Seminole County. (French, Hall). MISSISSIPPI - Damaging cotton in most counties with infestations of 5-7 percent; in 20 fields in Warren and Issaquena Counties. (Sartor). Larvae throughout delta counties. Heavy in spots, usually associated with weed host before moving into cotton. (Pfrimmer et al.). ARIZONA - Appearing in Pinal and Maricopa Counties. (Ariz. Coop. Sur.).

COTTON LEAF PERFORATOR (Bucculatrix thurberiella) - ARIZONA - Controls satisfactory at Yuma, Yuma County. Infestations developing at Gila Bend, Maricopa County. (Ariz. Coop. Sur.).

PLANT BUGS - ARIZONA - Lygus spp. numerous in Maricopa and Pinal Counties. Over 60 per 100 sweeps in 3 fields; treated. Adults averaged 3.38 per 100 sweeps and nymphs averaged 3.23 per 100 sweeps at Safford, Graham County. (Ariz. Coop. Sur.). MISSISSIPPI - Neurocolpus nubilus and Lygus lineolaris (tarnished plant bug) principal species present in northeast areas. Present in economic numbers in some untreated fields. Treatments applied. (Lincoln, Barnes). TENNESSEE - Light injury from L. lineolaris on pin head squares in rank cotton. (Locke).

COTTON FLEAHOPPER (Pseudatomoscelis seriatus) - TEXAS - Generally causing little concern in High Plains due to good fruit set of most cotton; however, in some areas, cotton still not setting sufficient fruit. Medium to heavy in Lynn County. (Almand, Clymer, Aug. 5).

SPIDER MITES (Tetranychus spp.) - TENNESSEE - Continue to increase; conditions ideal for further increase in western areas. (Locke).

TOBACCO

TOBACCO FLEA BEETLE (Epitrix hirtipennis) - WEST VIRGINIA - Adults light, 5 per plant on 10 tobacco plants in Lincoln County. (Hacker). VIRGINIA - Damage increasing on tobacco in Pittsylvania County. (Dominick). Generally low in flue-cured tobacco growing areas. (Rowell). Two fields with 12-20 holes per leaf on 95 percent of plants in Halifax County. (Allen).

POTATOES, TOMATOES, PEPPERS

GRANULATE CUTWORM (Feltia subterranea) - ALABAMA - About 10-15 percent of potato crop on 7,000+ acres in De Kalb County to be harvested as of August 1. Larval damage heavy. (Robinson).

POTATO TUBERWORM (Phthorimaea operculella) - MICHIGAN - In all areas surveyed no evidence of larvae feeding in any of 12 potato fields. Small residual population in some storage areas. (Newman, Aug. 4).

BEANS AND PEAS

MEXICAN BEAN BEETLE (Epilachna varivestis) - COLORADO - Larvae and adults continue to damage beans in Morgan, Weld, Larimer, and Boulder Counties. Controls applied; damage very light to heavy. (Johnson). WYOMING - Averaged 0-21 per bean plant in Platte, Goshen, and Laramie Counties. Pupae in few fields. Some controls applied. (Parshall).

COLE CROPS

IMPORTED CABBAGEWORM (Pieris rapae) - WISCONSIN - Controlled on cabbage in Outagamie and Columbia Counties. Egg being laid but averaged about 2 per leaf, low compared to some years. (Wis. Ins. Sur.). CALIFORNIA - This and Plutella xylostella (diamondback moth) caused heavy leaf damage to horseradish at Marysville, Yuba County. (Cal. Coop. Rpt.).

CABBAGE LOOPER (Trichoplusia ni) - NEW YORK - Increasing across State from Long Island to Western areas. On Long Island eggs found easily and in increasing numbers. (N.Y. Wkly. Rpt., Aug. 4).

CUCURBITS

CABBAGE LOOPER (Trichoplusia ni) - MARYLAND - Second to fourth-instar larvae causing serious rind injury to 5 acres of watermelons near Salisbury, Wicomico County. (U. Md., Ent. Dept.).

GENERAL VEGETABLES

CABBAGE LOOPER (Trichoplusia ni) - ARIZONA - Newly emerging lettuce requiring frequent treatment in Salt River Valley in Maricopa County. (Ariz. Coop. Sur.).

ONION MAGGOT (Hylemya antiqua) - COLORADO - Larvae ranged 0-1 per onion plant, with 20-30 percent of plants infested in Greeley and Kersey area of Weld County. (Johnson).

CORRECTIONS

CEIR 19(28):529 - A PHANTHOM MIDGE ... Collected by R.R. Rodgers ... should read Collected by R.R. Rogers ...

CEIR 19(28):530 - CEREAL LEAF BEETLE ... PENNSYLVANIA - ... in Highland Township, Elk County, should be Spring Creek Township, Elk County.

CEIR 19(29):537 - Detection ... APHID in Utah (p. 553) should be page 551.

CEIR 19(30):577 - SPIDER MITES ... RHODE ISLAND - ... T. cinnabarinus (carmine spider mite) should read T. urticae (two-spotted spider mite).

CEIR 19(31):595 - CHINCH BUG (Blissus leucopterus) should read SOUTHERN CHINCH BUG (Blissus insularis).

CEIR 19(32):629 - FACE FLY - Delete first entry for Missouri credited to Dinkins.

DECIDUOUS FRUITS AND NUTS

CODLING MOTH (Laspeyresia pomonella) - NEW MEXICO - Heavily infested (85-100 percent) untreated apples in San Juan County orchards. (Heninger). COLORADO - Second-brood adults in attractant traps in Mesa, Delta, Montrose, and Garfield Counties. Third and fourth cover sprays completed in 4-county area. (Bulla). WISCONSIN - Catch of 10 in blacklight trap at Madison, Dane County. (Wis. Ins. Sur.). MICHIGAN - Most larvae third to half grown. Pupation could begin in 7-10 days. Occasional adult (straggler or early second generation) appearing. (Thompson, Aug. 4).

ORIENTAL FRUIT MOTH (Grapholitha molesta) - COLORADO - Adults increased July 17-20 at Palisade, Mesa County. Flight peaked July 20. Up to 100 moths in 5 traps per day. Controls used where counts high. (Bulla). Two to 5 adults, up to 122 adults per 5 traps, week of July 20-26 at Vineland, Mesa County. Probably peak of second summer generation. (Sisson, Anderson).

PEACH TWIG BORER (Anarsia lineatella) - CALIFORNIA - Larvae heavy; damaged peach fruit at San Jose, Santa Clara County. (Cal. Coop. Rpt.).

YELLOW-NECKED CATERPILLAR (Datana ministra) - WASHINGTON - Damaged apple foliage at Ephrata and Quincy, Grant County. (Foeppel).

JUNE BEETLES (Cotinis spp.) - NEVADA - One male and 2 females of C. texana collected in bird repellent netting on nectarine tree at Las Vegas, Clark County. (Williams). Previously known in State only from female collected on rose at Las Vegas in 1967. (Bechtel, Aug. 1). OKLAHOMA - C. nitida (green June beetle) damage heavy to ripening peaches in Major and Blaine Counties. (Okla. Coop. Sur.).

APPLE MAGGOT (Rhagoletis pomonella) - MICHIGAN - Fly and egg laying activity increased. Fly emergence should peak in southwestern area orchards by August 15. Emergence should peak in 2 weeks in Upstate areas. (Thompson, Aug. 4). WISCONSIN - Heaviest catch of 53 flies on apple at Germantown, Washington County. (Wis. Ins. Sur.).

PEAR PSYLLA (Psylla pyricola) - OREGON - Unusually abundant in commercial pear orchards in Willamette Valley. Particularly troublesome where dormant season sprays neglected. (Every). MICHIGAN - Eggs increasing in unsprayed pear plots, sign of another generation. (Thompson, Aug. 4). RHODE ISLAND - Heavy and isolated in Washington County. (Field).

SPIDER MITES - OREGON - Panonychus ulmi (European red mite) building up in Willamette Valley apple orchards. (Every). NEVADA - Tetranychus sp. heavy on fruiting and ornamental peach at Reno and Sparks, Washoe County. (Ting, Aug. 1). COLORADO - T. urticae (two-spotted spider mite) heavy in apple and pear orchards in Mesa County and part of Delta County. Ranged 25-200 per leaf, controls applied. (Bulla). NEW MEXICO - T. mcdanieli moderate to heavy; damaged apple foliage in San Juan County apple orchards. Controls difficult. (Albert). NEW YORK - More apparent, not in large numbers, on peaches August 4 in Niagara County. (N.Y. Wkly. Rpt.).

PEAR RUST MITE (Epitrimerus pyri) - MICHIGAN - Immatures and adults in some pear blocks at Fennville, Allegan County. (Thompson, Aug. 4).

WALNUT CATERPILLAR (Datana integerrima) - OHIO - Larvae on walnut last 2-3 weeks. Very heavy, 90 percent defoliation, at Wooster, Wayne County. Larvae nearly full grown and parasitized by an ichneumon wasp, Anomalon sp. (Richter).

PECAN WEEVIL (Curculio caryae) - OKLAHOMA - Adult emergence very light in Okfuskee County. (Okla. Coop. Sur.).

WALNUT HUSK FLY (Rhagoletis completa) - CALIFORNIA - Emergence medium to heavy. Control started August 1 in northern area. (Cal. Coop. Rpt.).

CITRUS

Citrus Insect Situation in Florida - End of July - CITRUS RUST MITE (Phyllocoptruta oleivora) infested 86 (norm 63) percent of groves; 71 (norm 44) percent economic. Highest in 18 years of record in July. During last half of July infested average of 37.4 percent of leaves and 41.7 percent of fruit in groves that had not received a miticide 30 days prior to counting. Little change expected until downward trend develops about mid-August. All districts high. TEXAS CITRUS MITE (Eutetranychus banksi) infested 44 (norm 69) percent of groves; 30 (norm 43) percent economic. Below normal and moderate. Few heavy infestations will occur until decrease becomes general in September. Highest district central. CITRUS RED MITE (Panonychus citri) infested 53 (norm 63) percent of groves; 27 (norm 36) percent economic. Below normal and in moderate range. Decrease to low range expected in September. Very few heavy infestations will develop during next 2 months. Highest district north. GLOVER SCALE (Lepidosaphes gloverii) infested 79 (norm 76) percent of groves; 14 (norm 26) percent economic. Slightly below normal and in moderate range. Decrease expected after mid-August. Highest districts north and south. PURPLE SCALE (L. beckii) infested 57 (norm 68) percent of groves; 5 (norm 6) percent economic. Below normal and low, with little change expected in all districts. CHAFF SCALE (Parlatoria pergandii) infested 41 (norm 57) percent of groves; 4 (norm 6) percent economic. All districts subnormal and will remain low. YELLOW SCALE (Aonidiella citrina) infested 67 (norm 63) percent of groves; 9 (norm 8) percent economic. Near normal and decreasing. Very few infestations will be important. Highest districts north and central. BLACK SCALE (Saissetia oleae) infested 85 (norm 81) percent of groves; 64 (norm 63) percent economic. At normal high level. Although downward trend will become more evident by mid-August, population will continue in high range for another month. All districts high. An ARMORED SCALE (Unaspis citri) infested 21 percent of groves; moderate to heavy in 9 percent. Higher than in any prior month. Little change expected. WHITEFLIES infested 71 percent of groves; 34 percent economic. Decreased but still above normal and expected to remain high until mid-August. Highest districts east, central, and north. MEALYBUGS infested 82 percent of groves; 31 percent economic. Will continue above normal and in high range. Downward trend underway, should drop populations to moderate level before September. Highest districts east, south, and central. (W.A. Simanton (Citrus Expt. Sta., Lake Alfred)).

A LEAF ROLLER MOTH (Platynota stultana) - ARIZONA - Treatment required in nursery at Yuma, Yuma County. (Ariz. Coop. Sur.).

CITRUS THRIPS (Scirtothrips citri) - ARIZONA - Treatments continue in nurseries to protect young growth at Yuma, Yuma County. (Ariz. Coop. Sur.).

FLORIDA WAX SCALE (Ceroplastes floridensis) - FLORIDA - On 75 percent of 154 calamondin plants inspected at Mt. Plymouth, Lake County, August 1. (Bentley).

CITRUS FLAT MITE (Brevipalpus lewisi) - ARIZONA - Tangerine grove required fruit protection at Yuma, Yuma County. (Ariz. Coop. Sur.).

OTHER TROP. & SUBTROP. FRUITS

FIG PSYLLID (Homotoma ficus) - CALIFORNIA - Very light in 8 by 10-mile area around Concord, Contra Costa County. Indications are that this pest capable of extremely heavy populations at least in coastal areas. (Cal. Coop. Rpt.).

OMNIVOROUS LOOPER (Sabulodes caberata) - CALIFORNIA - Damaged avocado foliage at Bonsall, San Diego County. (Cal. Coop. Rpt.).

ORNAMENTALS

BAGWORM (Thyridopteryx ephemeraeformis) - ALABAMA - Killing many cedar, arborvitae, and other shrubs in Chambers, Madison, Greene, and other counties. (Pigott et al.).

SOFT SCALES - OREGON - Pulvinaria floccifera still severe on camellia at Corvallis, Benton County. Biological control ineffective. (Westcott). WEST VIRGINIA - Neolecanium cornuparvum (magnolia scale) heavy on Harrison County magnolia. (Cole).

A LACE BUG (Stephanitis takeyai) - RHODE ISLAND - Very heavy in some nurseries in Washington County. (Field).

FOREST AND SHADE TREES

PINE NEEDLE SCALE (Phenacaspis pinifoliae) - WISCONSIN - More than half hatched on Rock County spruce August 1; about half exposed on new growth. (Wis. Ins. Sur.).

COOLEY SPRUCE GALL APHID (Adelges cooleyi) - WISCONSIN - Hatched on Douglas-fir in southeastern area. (Wis. Ins. Sur.).

RED-HEADED PINE SAWFLY (Neodiprion lecontei) - VERMONT - Appears to have fallen off in 1969. No infestations to date. (Nielsen, Aug. 6).

WHITE-MARKED TUSSOCK MOTH (Hemerocampa leucostigma) - ILLINOIS - Heavy on Cook County elms in about 100 acres along streets. Larvae, pupae, and wingless females present. Pupae solidly cover lower 20 feet of some trees. Some trees show 50 percent defoliation. (Ill. Ins. Rpt.).

MOURNING-CLOAK BUTTERFLY (Nymphalis antiopa) - NEVADA - Larvae heavy on elms and willows at Reno and Sparks, Washoe County, and Lovelock, Pershing County. (Wesley, Ferraro).

FALL WEBWORM (Hyphantria cunea) - WISCONSIN - Infestation normal in central area; present in Outagamie and Oconto Counties. (Wis. Ins. Sur.). OHIO - Occurred sporadically since June. Distribution of overwintered webs this spring indicates high numbers this fall in southeastern area, especially in Jefferson, Harrison, and Belmont Counties. (Richter). MASSACHUSETTS - Small webs first seen August 1 in Hampshire County. (Mankowsky).

A PLANT BUG (Tropidosteptes pacificus) - OREGON - Defoliation extensive to about 2,500 ash trees 3 to 4 years old in nursery at Portland, Multnomah County. Nymphs and adults present. (Nicolaison).

MAN AND ANIMALS

SCREW-WORM (Cochliomyia hominivorax) - One case reported in U.S. August 3-9 as follows: CALIFORNIA - San Diego County. Total of 129 laboratory-confirmed cases reported in portion of Barrier Zone in Republic of Mexico July 27 to August 2 as follows: Baja California 1, Sonora 52, Chihuahua 61, Nuevo Leon 5, Tamaulipas 10. Total of 19 cases reported in Mexico south of Barrier Zone. Barrier Zone is area where eradication operation underway to prevent establishment of self-sustaining population in U.S. Sterile screw-worm flies released: Texas 45,568,000; New Mexico 4,360,000; Arizona 10,720,000; California 700,000; Mexico 104,440,000. (Anim. Health Div.).

HORN FLY (Haematobia irritans) - MARYLAND - Ranged 0-50 per head of dairy cattle in Frederick, Carroll, and Howard Counties. (U. Md., Ent. Dept.). ILLINOIS - Average per head of cattle by district: Southeast 547.3, west-southwest 153.5, and southwest 3.0. (Ill. Ins. Rpt.). ALABAMA - Unusual; no large numbers on cattle in Greene, Hale, Marengo, Perry, Montgomery, Macon, and Lee Counties. (Johnson et al.). MISSISSIPPI - None on 500 treated cattle in Monroe County; averaged 250

er head on 500 untreated cattle. Averaged 18 per head on 168 Hinds County cattle.
Sartor). OKLAHOMA - Moderate to heavy on Nowata County cattle. (Okla. Coop. Sur.).

TABLE FLY (Stomoxys calcitrans) - ILLINOIS - Average per head of cattle by
istrict: West-southwest 21.8, southwest 14.0, southeast 11.0, and northwest 0.6.
Ill. Ins. Rpt.).

ACE FLY (Musca autumnalis) - VERMONT - Severe in some areas of State. (Nielsen,
ug. 6). MARYLAND - Ranged 1-28 per face on cattle in Frederick, Carroll, and
oward Counties. (U. Md., Ent. Dept.). OHIO - Remains low to moderate, averaged
0-20 per face, on dairy cattle in most of northeastern area. (Richter).
LLINOIS - Averaged per face on cattle by district: West-southwest 25.8, southeast
3.3, southwest 10.6, and northwest 6.1. (Ill. Ins. Rpt.). ARKANSAS - Absent in
2 western counties. (Lancaster et al.). CALIFORNIA - Continues to spread. Light
n Lake and Plumas Counties for new county records. First shipment of pupae of a
redaceous staphylinid beetle, Aleochara tristis, distributed to Shasta and
umboldt Counties; about 70 percent emergence occurred. (Cal. Coop. Rpt.).
ASHINGTON - Low, less than 4 per face, in Klickitat, Benton, and Yakima Counties;
lightly higher on Whitman County beef herds. (Telford).

OSQUITOES - MARYLAND - Aedes vexans expected to increase rapidly statewide due to
eavy flooding of past weeks. (U. Md., Ent. Dept.). OHIO - Control programs in 8
ortheastern counties reduced adults. Larvae in Wayne County remain high,
specially Anopheles. About 200 bites per hour east of New Philadelphia, Tuscara-
as County; 80 adults collected in 5-10 minutes; nearly all Aedes trivittatus.
Richter). WISCONSIN - Subsided past few days; numbers still ample. (Wis. Ins.
ur.). MINNESOTA - Decline steady since peak week ending July 18 at Minneapolis
nd St. Paul. Of 4,924 females in 16 light traps week ending August 1, A. vexans
,527. Mansonia perturbans down to 737 females. Larval and bite collections down.
Minn. Pest Rpt.). CALIFORNIA - Remain high. Marked increase of Culex tarsalis
ince June, particularly in remote parts of northern area, Sacramento Valley,
outhern San Joaquin Valley, Owens Valley, and limited parts of southern area.
arvae still increasing; but control programs within communities kept numbers
ormal. Full State emergency program implemented in July in uncontrolled areas and
einforced areas under local control. Intensive surveillance for encephalitis in
orses revealed 3 presumptive positive cases of western equine encephalitis, based
n serologic tests. (Cal. Coop. Rpt.).

OMMON CATTLE GRUB (Hypoderma lineatum) - ALABAMA - Laying eggs in Montgomery
ounty beef herd as evidenced by stamping of cattle. (McCabe et al.).

ULICID FLEAS - OKLAHOMA - Compared with other ectoparasites on dogs, Cteno-
ephalides felis (cat flea) and Pulex simulans occurred in heaviest averages on
ost of 93 dogs checked in pounds at Enid (Garfield County), Ponca City (Kay
ounty), Stillwater (Payne County), Guthrie (Logan County), and Edmond (Oklahoma
ounty). C. felis averaged 39 per infested dog on 58 dogs, P. simulans averaged
.8 per infested dog on 47 dogs. (Okla. Coop. Sur.).

IOUSEHOLDS AND STRUCTURES

. DERMESTID BEETLE (Anthrenus coloratus) - NEW MEXICO - Collected in tack room at
unland Park race track in Dona Ana County by B. Campbell and C. Seagraves June 16.
etermined by C.J. Hansel. This is a new State record. (N.M. Coop. Rpt.).

UROPEAN EARWIG (Forficula auricularia) - PENNSYLVANIA - Collected in home in
ioga County August 6 for a new county record. (Gesell).

ENEFICIAL INSECTS

. GREEN LACEWING (Chrysopa sp.) - WYOMING - Adults and larvae numerous on alfalfa
nd corn in southeastern area. Averaged 20 per 10 sweeps in Converse County alfalfa
ield. (Parshall).

FEDERAL AND STATE PLANT PROTECTION PROGRAMS

BOLL WEEVIL (Anthonomus grandis) - TEXAS - Up to about 1,500 adults per acre in
majority of Dickens and Kent County cotton fields. Punctured 5-45 percent of
squares in Borden County. Light in Scurry County. (Almand, Clymer, Aug. 5). For
Boll Weevil in other areas see page 643.

CEREAL LEAF BEETLE (Oulema melanopus) - ILLINOIS - Adults light on oats at Hay-
worth, McLean County, for a new county record. Collected by O.E. Warnke August
7. Determined by R.E. White. (PPC).

GRASSHOPPERS - WASHINGTON - Melanoplus sanguinipes economic on private and State
rangeland by county: Asotin 960 acres, Garfield 1,600 acres, and Whitman 640
acres. (Nonini, Nishimura). OREGON - Mostly M. sanguinipes adults averaging up to
12 per square yard west of Chenoweth near The Dalles, Wasco County, and damaging
gardens. (Larson et al.). CALIFORNIA - Bruneria shastana and Bradynotes obesa
heavy on 500 acres of Jeffrey pine at Doe Peak, Siskiyou County; treated August 5.
(Cal. Coop. Rpt.). NEW MEXICO - Heavy; damaged rangeland along Cimarron River
near Folsom; most severe in extreme southern part of Union County; spotted and
heavy along east side of county. (Zimmerman). WYOMING - Total of 204,111 acres
sprayed in Converse, Goshen, and Platte Counties; 95+ percent effective. (Patch).
NEBRASKA - M. differentialis and M. femurrubrum dominant. Ranged 25-80 per square
yard in Jefferson and Otoe Counties and 10-15 per square yard in Buffalo and
Merrick Counties. Some injury to adjacent row crops. (Roselle). MISSOURI -
Melanoplus sp. feeding on white oak, hickory, and dogwood on about 300 acres in
Iron County; defoliated 40 percent of trees. (Gass).

GYPSY MOTH (Porthetria dispar) - PENNSYLVANIA - Adults collected for new county
records. At Mifflinburg in Union County by T. MacDonald July 18. In West Beaver
Township, Snyder County, by R. Strahl July 22. In Armagh Township, Mifflin County,
by D.M. Bowman July 22. In Greenwood Township, Juniata County, by A. Varner July
25. Determined by R.W. Hodges. In Washington Township, York County, by D.L. Reiter
July 29. In Hamiltonban Township, Adams County, by R.T. Shafer July 31. Determined
by E.L. Todd. (PPC). NEW YORK - Pupal cases and egg clusters mainly at Shoreham,
Rocky Point, Wading River, and Riverhead in Suffolk County. (N.Y. Wkly. Rpt.,
Aug. 4). VERMONT - Adults active; egg masses in some areas of State. (Nielsen,
Aug. 6). RHODE ISLAND - Eggs laid in Providence County August 1. Eggs still laid
in Washington County. (Relli, Stelle).

IMPORTED FIRE ANT (Solenopsis saevissima richteri) - GEORGIA - Adults collected in
Appling County July 21 and Toombs County July 22 by Moore and Camp for new county
records. Determined by D.R. Smith. (PPC).

JAPANESE BEETLE (Popillia japonica) - MARYLAND - Adult injury averaged 10 percent
in 20-acre soybean field at Princess Anne, Somerset County. Adults damaged 10
percent of silks in 35-acre cornfield near Lisbon, Howard County. (U. Md., Ent.
Dept.). PENNSYLVANIA - Feeding on grapes, corn silks, potatoes, and poison ivy in
Greene County August 2. (Dinsmore). OHIO - Chewing silks off corn in many southern
and central areas. Five to 10 adults per ear not uncommon where counts high. Too
late to interfere with pollination of early corn but high enough to potentially
threaten late-planted corn. Defoliated Butler County soybeans. (Zorn). KENTUCKY -
Adults light for new county records. On rosebush at Manchester, Clay County, by
H. Hurst July 9. On sassafras and oak in Mammoth Cave National Park in Edmonson
County by S. Harn August 7. Determined by L.K. Russell. (PPC).

PINK BOLLWORM (Pectinophora gossypiella) - CALIFORNIA - Catch of 16,378 native and
2,883 sterile moths in Coachella Valley August 1-6. Native population increasing in
spite of sterile releases. Collection of 131 full-grown larvae from 68 of 9,070
cotton bolls, relatively low in view of adult catch. Sterile releases: Coachella
Valley 408,200; Kern County 82,500; Borrego Springs 115,800. Total to date respec-
tively: 11,292,980; 260,660; 987,550. (PPC). ARIZONA - Light numbers more evident
in Salt River Valley, Maricopa County. Infested 2-3 of every 100 cotton bolls at
Safford, Graham County. (Ariz. Coop. Sur.). TEXAS - Catch of 3,094 moths in blacklight traps in McLennan and Falls Counties. (Cowan et al.).

RANGE CATERPILLAR (Hemileuca oliviae) - NEW MEXICO - Hatch began week ending July
18 on about 100 sections of rangeland in Lincoln County. (Dunlap). Currently heavy;
damaged grass north and south of Clayton, south of Mt. Dora, and in entire area
around Sofia in Union County. (Zimmerman).

PISTACHIO SEED CHALCID (Megastigmus pistaciae) - CALIFORNIA - Another infestation
in wild "escape trees" within 1 mile of Plant Introduction Station at Chico, Butte
County. (PPC). Adults trapped outside the station in ornamental Chinese pistachio
(Pistacia chinensis) trees in immediate area. Eradication effort continues. (Cal.
Coop. Rpt.).

SOYBEAN CYST NEMATODE (Heterodera glycines) - MISSISSIPPI - Cysts collected for
new county records. At Ruleville, Sunflower County, by Holett and others July 16.
At Marietta, Prentiss County, by G.M. Wilson July 25. Determined by W. Friedman.
(PPC).

WHITE-FRINGED BEETLES (Graphognathus spp.) - GEORGIA - Adults light in Seminole
County. (Hall, French). TENNESSEE - Adults light in vacant lot of home at Hohen-
wald, Lewis County, for a new county record. Collected by H.L. Robinson July 14.
Determined by J.M. Kingsolver. (PPC). Infestations reported in Lincoln, Wayne,
Fayette, and Davidson Counties. (Stamey et al.). ARKANSAS - G. leucoloma striatus
adults moderate on white clover adjacent to school at Newport, Jackson County, for
a new county record. Collected by E. Moore and F. Prentice July 31. Determined by
R.E. Warner. (PPC).

INSECT DETECTION

New State Records - A WEEVIL (Onychobaris depressa) - ARIZONA - Adults collected
on airplane wing at Yuma, Yuma County, by D.M. Tuttle May 15, 1964. (Ariz. Coop.
Sur.). Hosts in family Compositae. (PPC). A DERMESTID BEETLE (Anthrenus coloratus)
NEW MEXICO - Dona Ana County (p. 649).

New County Records - ASIATIC OAK WEEVIL (Cyrtepistomus castaneus) MISSOURI -
Carter, Howell (p. 641). CEREAL LEAF BEETLE (Oulema melanopus) ILLINOIS -
McLean (p. 650). CLOVER HEAD WEEVIL (Hypera meles) MISSOURI - Macon, Marion,
Ralls (p. 641). CLOVER SEED WEEVIL (Miccotrogus picirostris) MISSOURI -
Chariton, Howard, Lincoln, Macon, Marion, Monroe, Pike (p. 641). EUROPEAN EARWIG
(Forficula auricularia) PENNSYLVANIA - Tioga (p. 649). FACE FLY (Musca autumnalis)
CALIFORNIA - Lake, Plumas (p. 649). GYPSY MOTH (Porthetria dispar) PENNSYLVANIA -
Adams, Juniata, Mifflin, Snyder, Union, York (p. 650). IMPORTED FIRE ANT (Solenop-
sis saevissima richteri) GEORGIA - Appling, Toombs (p. 650). JAPANESE BEETLE
(Popillia japonica) KENTUCKY - Clay, Edmonson (p. 650). A JAPANESE WEEVIL
(Calomycterus setarius) - MISSOURI - Marion (p. 642). MEADOW SPITTLEBUG (Philaenus
spumarius) MISSOURI - Chariton (p. 642). SOYBEAN CYST NEMATODE (Heterodera gly-
cines) MISSISSIPPI - Prentiss, Sunflower (p. 651). WHITE-FRINGED BEETLES
(Graphognathus spp.) TENNESSEE - Lewis; ARKANSAS - G. leucoloma striatus in
Jackson (p. 651).

HAWAII INSECT REPORT

Pastures - A GRASS WEBWORM (Herpetogramma licarsisalis) caused moderate to heavy damage in Kikuyu grass pastures at high elevations in Pahoa and Central Kona District, Hawaii Island. Larvae 20-25 per square foot at Pahoa, 10-12 at Kona; adults and eggs light; larval parasites, Eucelatoria armigera (a tachina fly) and Casinaria infesta (an ichneumon wasp), very noticeable. Larvae heavy; damage moderate and spotty in 100+ acres of Kikuyu grass at Hana, Maui. Adults heavy in pastures; 90 percent of eggs parasitized by Trichogramma semifumatum (a minute egg parasite); larval parasites light. In certain sections of Kalaheo, Kauai, larvae averaging 17 per square foot in Kikuyu grass pastures; adults moderate on wayside vegetation; 58 eggs parasitized out of 76 collected. (Yoshioka et al.).

General Vegetables - CARMINE SPIDER MITE (Tetranychus cinnabarinus), GREENHOUSE WHITEFLY (Trialeurodes vaporariorum), and LEAF MINER FLIES (Liriomyza spp.) increasing in all farming areas on Oahu. Severe in many snap bean fields. T. cinnabarinus and leaf miner flies heavy in most watermelon fields. Mites heavy to severe on eggplant, corn, daikon, Chinese squash, and pumpkin. Whiteflies heavy to severe in some fields of bittermelon and cucumber. Leaf miner flies moderate to heavy in many fields of green onions, mustard cabbage, tomato, Chinese squash, daikon, and yard-long beans. Difficult to control despite intensive spraying. (Yamamoto et al.). All stages of GREEN PEACH APHID (Myzus persicae) severe on eggplants at Punaluu and Pearl City, Oahu; adults and/or nymphs 50-650 per leaf. (Funasaki).

Ornamentals - All stages of PALM MEALYBUG (Palmicultor palmarum) moderate on terminals of 75 out of 150 young potted coconut trees in nursery at Koko Head, Oahu. (Funasaki, Kawamura). A NOCTUID MOTH (Melipotis ochrodes) increasing in several areas on Oahu. Adults heavy in brush areas amid kiawe thickets; damage to kiawe foliage conspicuous on some trees on Sand Island. Adults heavy in brushy areas at Ewa, airport area, and Waianae. Blacklight trap at Animal Quarantine Station in Honolulu caught 57 adults. (Au).

Man and Animals - MOSQUITOES - Catch of 109 Aedes vexans nocturnus and 4,308 Culex pipiens quinquefasciatus from 53 light traps on Oahu in July. Aedes catches remain low in all areas. Culex counts highest at Nanakuli and Waipahu. (Mosq. Contr. Br., Dept. of Health).

Beneficial Insects - Several hundred larvae of a LADY BEETLE (Cryptolaemus montrouzieri) on outer walls of homes at Kaneohe, Oahu. Larvae heavy on nearby fiddlewood trees infested with 1-20 immature forms of BARNACLE SCALE (Ceroplastes cirripediformis) per leaf. (Kawamura). LANTANA HISPID (Uroplata girardi) larvae and adults heavy in 5 acres of lantana at Waihee, Maui. Heavy larval damage on about 75 percent of leaves. Newly emerged adults very abundant on plants. (Ah Sam).

LIGHT TRAP COLLECTIONS

Location / Date	Temp. Range °F	Precip. (in)	Type of trap	Trichoplusia ni (cabbage looper)	Spodoptera frugiperda (fall armyworm)	Spodoptera exigua (beet armyworm)	Heliothis zea and/or virescens	Prodenia ornithogalli (yellow-striped armyworm)	Peridroma saucia (variegated cutworm)	sp.	Agrotis malefida	Mamestra configurata	Pseudaletia unipuncta (armyworm)	webworm sp.	Feltia subterranea (granulate cutworm)	army cutworm	Euxoa sp.	other (no. + species)
FLORIDA																		
Gainesville 8/1-7			BL		36	31		5		1	1		39	1	17	3		
MINNESOTA																		
Crookston 8/1-7				1			25			5							18	12
Fergus Falls 8/1-7				3			1			1							21	4
Rochester 8/1-7				3			27										1	4
Worthington 8/1-7							1			4							3	4
MISSISSIPPI																		
Stoneville 8/2-8	63-94	none	2BL	372	57	583	20	217		2	2		592	16	17	67		16
MISSOURI																		
Fair Grove 7/31-8/6							43	80	2	42			19					62
NEW JERSEY																		
Cedarville 7/28-8/4			BL	86	1		37	33	4	7		9	6					21
Evesboro 7/28-8/4			BL	14			42	41	8	18		8	11					10
Halltown 7/28-8/4			BL	38			8	23	7	8		66						9
Plainsboro 7/28-8/4				43			53	9	5	19		6	4					2
TEXAS																		
Waco 8/2-8	77-100	0.2		1733	37	109	27	21	1				300	25	53			6
WISCONSIN																		
Madison 8/1-6			BL				8											3

Distribution of Brown Recluse Spider

Loxosceles reclusa

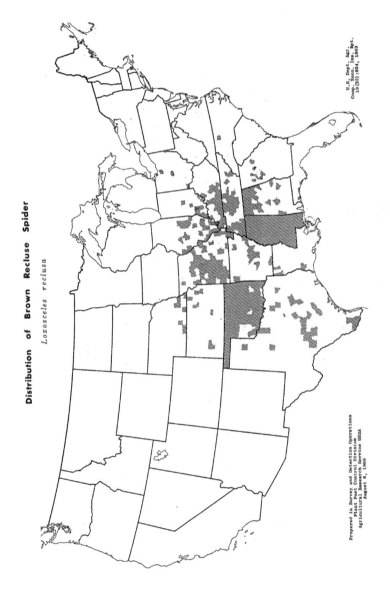

Prepared in Survey and Detection Operations
Plant Pest Control Division
Agricultural Research Service USDA
August 8, 1969

U.S. Dept. Agr.
Coop. Econ. Ins. Rpt.
19 (33):654, 1969

CPSIA information can be obtained
at www.ICGtesting.com
Printed in the USA
BVHW031145021118
531990BV00020B/1373/P